In Praise of Julie Hliboki's Books

Breathing Light: Accompanying Loss and Grief with Love and Gratitude

"*Breathing Light* is the kind of book that we have grown to expect from the mind and pen of Julie Hliboki. It is both visual and narrative in form; it is simple without being simplistic; and it offers a way of dealing with those issues that eventually confront us all—aging, suffering and death. This book may just have the wisdom for which you have been seeking."

—**Ben C. Johnson**, Professor Emeritus, Columbia Theological Seminary

"If you encounter loss in life—as a companion to others, sitting beside a loved one, or facing the approach of your own—you will find Julie Hliboki's book, *Breathing Light*, an inspiration. Breathe in and feel your pain held and known; breathe out sustained and buoyant with hope."

—**Frank Rogers Jr., Ph.D.**, Director, Center for Engaged Compassion at Claremont School of Theology, and author of *Practicing Compassion*

"Julie Hliboki's writings will bring guidance and calm to the important work of being with people in difficult times. *Breathing Light* will help anyone seeking to be graceful in providing good care."

—**John Calvi**, author of *The Dance Between Hope and Fear*

The Breath of God: Thirty-Three Invitations to Embody Holy Wisdom

"Here is a contemporary and inspired presentation of the Names of God. They are presented in various creative modalities to inspire the reader in his/her own spiritual journey in the world. These are the beautiful divine names that will enlighten the seeker."

—**Aziza Scott**, head of the Esoteric School, Sufi Order International

"This wise book reveals of deep interfaith appre and a master teacher of

—**Robert McDerm** of Integral Studies and Editor of *The New Essential Steiner*

"*The Breath of God*, written and compiled by Julie Hliboki, is a devotional poetic reflection on the most beautiful Names of God, offered through the language of personal experience bringing words together with beautiful artistry creating devotional songs based on the Monotheistic tradition. Dr. Hliboki's poetic reflections bring the reader together with the seeking heart of the wayfarer, a heart that sees beauty in all that exists, experiences divine in every reflection, appreciates the bounty and richness that she has received from the generosity of the Being, yet expressed in a contemporary language for the modern reader."

—**Nahid Angha, Ph.D.**, Co-director of the International Association of Sufism and Executive Director of *Sufism Journal*

"As a teacher of contemplative practice, I am constantly reminded that most practices focus on only one dimension of experience—for example, the use of images rather than words. But Julie Hliboki moves past this narrowness, inviting us into a multi-dimensional contemplative experience. She draws on the wisdom of the Abrahamic spiritual paths to weave together processes of vocal, musical, and visual expression, as well as insights from the sacred words, texts, and sages. By allowing us to activate this full range of contemplative capacities, *The Breath of God* offers us a rare and much-needed experience: a profoundly integrated contemplative practice for the cultivation of a profoundly integrated life."

—**Andrew Dreitcer, Ph.D.**, Associate Professor of Spirituality and Director of the Center for Engaged Compassion, Claremont School of Theology

"*The Breath of God* is a beautiful book, visually and spiritually. As lovely as its artwork is, its rich mix of words and images takes us to the depths of something lovelier still, which many people call God, whose name is both known and unknown. This book moves as the human heart moves, between the seen and the unseen, and somehow embraces it all. Read this book meditatively, in the spirit with which it was written, and it will open your heart—to yourself, to others, and ultimately to the beauty behind this world of suffering and joy."

—**Parker J. Palmer**, author of *The Courage to Teach, A Hidden Wholeness, Let Your Life Speak*, and *Healing the Heart of Democracy*

"A stunning feast of the spirit, this book describes a pathway to God. Through stories of her personal journey, the author shows us how we can breathe God too. By drawing upon faith traditions, she shares wisdom of the ancients. We have been invited on the journey, accompanied every step of the way."

—**Frances Henry**, founder of Global Violence Prevention

Cultivating Compassion in an Interfaith World: 99 Meditations to Embrace the Beloved

"A wonderful comparison of the shared roots across religious traditions that lifts out the centrality of compassion. In concrete and inviting ways, *Cultivating Compassion in an Interfaith World* illustrates respect for each tradition while engaging the reader with creative suggestions to develop the practice of compassion within and across our traditions—a brilliant contribution to all of us concerned with finding ways to deepen our wells of kindness and build bridges across our many divides."

—**John Paul Lederach, Ph.D.**, Professor of International Peacebuilding, Kroc Institute, University of Notre Dame, author of *The Moral Imagination: The Art and Soul of Building Peace*

"Religions do not have a strong reputation for creating compassionate or inclusive people—despite the clear teachings of their founders. We often emphasize belief systems instead of practices that actually change our hearts, minds and behavior. In this excellent and much needed book, *Cultivating Compassion in an Interfaith World* will help bridge this gap."

—**Fr. Richard Rohr, O.F.M.**, Center for Action and Contemplation, author of *The Naked Now* and *Everything Belongs*

"The major premise of this book is simple: Compassion is essential for both personal and our collective well-being and happiness. Using meditation as the particular instrument of personal transformation, Hliboki integrates the wisdom of Eastern and Western religious traditions as she guides us through a process for deepening our capacity for compassion. In doing so she draws attention to the essential ingredients for a transformation of consciousness—finding our center; addressing our illusions; realizing our inter-connectedness with all being; and experiencing the divine essence that flows through our relationships with self, others and nature. This contemplative consciousness is the life force of a compassion that has the power to transform the human condition. Realizing it answers any question or doubt about our true purpose in life."

—**Robert G. Toth**, Past Executive Director, Merton Institute for Contemplative Living

"Hliboki has been blessed with a very precious spirituality, and she is, once again, moved to share it with us in a work that enriches the heart, mind, and soul. It is our prayer that God continues to bless her, and that she continues to publish these blessings."

—**Imam Plemon T. El-Amin**, Chair, Interfaith Community Initiatives

"This is a beautiful, simple and open-hearted guide to contemplative practice. It contains much practical wisdom and will provide real support and encouragement to those seeking to live with greater compassion."
—**Douglas E. Christie, Ph.D.**, Loyola Marymount University, author of *The Word in the Desert* and *The Blue Sapphire of the Mind*

"Like a prism of light, *Cultivating Compassion in an Interfaith World* refracts the pure light of the Beloved into a gorgeous spectrum of possibilities. These serve as portals to remind us of the inexplicable immediacy of Divine Presence. The genius of this book is not only its vision but also how it calls the reader to take up spiritual practices that open the mind and heart to the radiant light of compassion. Be forewarned—these practices not only console but also call us to stretch beyond our comfort zones, to become larger than ourselves so that we might become who we truly are."
—**Rev. Robert V. Thompson**, author of A Voluptuous God: A Christian Heretic Speaks

"*Cultivating Compassion in an Interfaith World* captures the essence of compassion from different spiritual traditions, showing us how common love is amongst all peoples. In spite of this, many people find it hard to practice compassion in their daily lives to others and to themselves. Hliboki's book presents practical contemplative spiritual exercises that can be easily taught to clinicians and others needing to integrate compassion into our own lives and helping them recognize the sacred in all we do. I strongly recommend this book to anyone searching for the sacred within and especially to those in the healing professions."
—**Christina M. Puchalski, MD**, Director, George Washington Institute for Spirituality and Health

"At a time when kindness may be interpreted as weakness, and when concern for others is often limited to messages in cyberspace, *Cultivating Compassion in an Interfaith World* demonstrates the beauty and peace that comes with an attitude of true compassion. Drawing from Islamic, Christian and Buddhist scriptures, it is a helpful resource for people of faith who wish to infuse their lives with the light of compassion."
—**Tayyibah Taylor**, Publisher & Editor-in-Chief, *Azizah Magazine*

"Hliboki writes with palpable respect for three of the major faith traditions, identifying common ground but cherishing their distinctiveness. Pastors, retreat leaders or spiritual mentors who value the diversity of religious experience ought to be able to utilize her book as a guide and resource with minimal adaptation for varying circumstances or audiences. Hliboki looks both East and West, and in her book the twain meet."
—**Alexander Patico**, North American Secretary, Orthodox Peace Fellowship

Also by the Author

The Breath of God:
Thirty-Three Invitations to Embody Holy Wisdom

Cultivating Compassion in an Interfaith World:
99 Meditations to Embrace the Beloved

Compassion Meditation Cards:
An Interfaith Approach to Cultivating Compassion —
For You, for Others, and for the World!

Replenish: Thirty-Three Openings to the Sacred

Breathing Light

Accompanying Loss and Grief with Love and Gratitude

Julie Hliboki

Photography by David Foster

To John Paul,
with love +
gratitude,
Julie Hliboki

Transilient Publishing

With Gratitude

It is such a joy for me to birth a book into being. I find the process nourishes my body, mind, and soul. The journey of creating *Breathing Light* has fed me for the past several years, beginning with accompanying people along the end of life path, and culminating in the book you hold in your hands.

Along the way, several generous and talented people helped shape *Breathing Light* into its final form. Patrick McComas furnished the beautiful graphic design and layout, Amy Ferguson and Cheri Tiernan imparted thoughtful edits, and Stephanie DiLorio delivered careful proofreading. Over many cups of tea, my good friend, David Foster, helped me think through the formation of *Breathing Light*. Matching his gorgeous nature photographs to my poems and essays was pure joy. I always felt happy after viewing his images.

I am thankful for the precious time with hospice and hospital patients, their families, and caregivers. I learn so much through every visit. I am also grateful for my beloved, David Addiss, who breathes Light with me everyday.

Contributors

Becca Holohan writes short stories and poems about living into one's essence. Her expressive works have been featured at interfaith gatherings, art exhibitions, and yoga retreats. Becca is working toward her teaching certification in yoga with the intent of blending movement with poetry.

Hazrat Inayat Khan (1882–1927) was a Sufi teacher from India who founded The Sufi Order in the West (now called Sufi Order International) in the early part of the twentieth century. His teaching strongly emphasizes the fundamental oneness of all religions. His published works include *The Inner Life* and *The Soul's Journey*.

Ian McCrorie is a longtime practitioner of meditation, has studied Buddhism worldwide, and teaches courses in Vipassana meditation. He is the author of *The Moon Appears When the Water is Still: Reflections of the Dhamma*.

James Dillet Freeman (1912–2003) was a minister of the Unity church and a poet. His 1941 "Prayer for Protection" was taken aboard Apollo 11 in July 1969 by Lunar Module pilot Buzz Aldrin.

>>

Kendall Dana Lockerman writes poetry and occasional prose that is sometimes theological. His published poems appear in two small volumes—*Seasons, Saints & Angels* and *Rain*.

Marian Monahan is a Spiritual Director and retreat leader who has written poetry all of her life. Themes center on nature, family, silence, and life's transitions—places where she finds the Beloved.

Mary Ann Downey is a member and former clerk of the Atlanta Friends Meeting. She shares Quaker beliefs through the Friends Traveling Ministry Program, and as director of Decision Bridges, which offers courses on the Quaker consensus decision process. Several of her essays have been published in *Friends Journal*.

Roshi Joan Halifax, Ph.D., is a Buddhist teacher, Zen priest, anthropologist, and pioneer in the field of end-of-life care. She is Founder, Abbot, and Head Teacher of Upaya Institute and Zen Center in Santa Fe, New Mexico. Her books include *Being With Dying: Cultivating Compassion and Wisdom in the Presence of Death*.

Steven J. Gold is the founder/director of the Yoga and Judaism Center. He is an initiate in a Himalayan meditation tradition, a student and practitioner of Kabala and Western mysticism. His books include *Yoga and Judaism, Explorations of a Jewish Yogi* and *IVRI: The Essence of Hebrew Spirituality, 21st Century Perspectives on an Ancient Tradition*.

Contents

About this Book

Breath is central to every living thing. Our in-breath connects the living world to us, and our out-breath connects us to the living world. Many spiritual traditions speak of breath as the essence of God, our connection to the Divine Spirit. For example, God's Old Testament name as Yahweh (or YHWY) is composed of aspirated consonants that, when spoken, sound like breathing. The word "spirit" comes from the Latin "spiritus," meaning breath. When we breathe, we are participating in the sacred oneness with all life.

In Quakerism (The Religious Society of Friends), and other religions, Light plays a key role in prayer and healing. As Friends, we hold someone in the Light (God's presence) to illumine a person, a situation, or a problem, whether in concern or thanksgiving. We often do this by first centering down into a physical, mental, and spiritual quietude.

I first conceived of *Breathing Light: Accompanying Loss and Grief with Love and Gratitude* during visits with hospice patients and their families. As a Quaker interfaith chaplain, before visiting with people, I would enter a short period of meditation to center myself. With focused attention on my breath, I held in the Light whoever was on the other side of the door. The attentiveness to breath aligned me with the Divine essence and prepared me to accept whoever and whatever awaited me. Once inside the room, conversation, prayers, silence, or further meditation would evolve.

As I accompanied people through the dying process, I recognized that their last breath released them into the radiance beyond. With some, I witnessed the actual transformation of their energy into luminosity. It occurred to me that at some point during the dying progression, in that liminal state of having a foot in both worlds, the departing person began the process of "breathing light."

My role in accompanying them through this end journey often included the contemplative practice of Tonglen—inhaling their pain to create spaciousness for them, and exhaling whatever would bring them relief and happiness. Through this meditation, I was able to help breathe them into luminosity. For the families, I offered the Metta (loving-kindness) meditation, a profoundly moving practice to cultivate forgiveness, compassion, and love, and to sense connection through breath. I taught healthcare workers both practices to help them center, address their anxiety and stress, and release so much of what they carry in their bodies. A description of the two meditations can be found at the end of this book.

Breathing Light is designed around the practices that create compassionate space for those we care about, including ourselves. The "Inhale" section includes poetry, essays, and prose written by me that speak to the many emotions we experience as a loved one makes his or her final journey. It is, in a sense, our willingness to breathe in suffering that allows us to be fully present to their experience.

Often as a chaplain, the first time I meet someone is when they are experiencing traumatic crisis—serious illness, dying, or death. In one moment we are strangers and in the next moment we are sharing sacred, vulnerable space. Many of the "Inhale" writings arose from these intimate moments. The other essays and poems reflect my own suffering and inspiration in God's presence. In order to share this work with you, I have changed names and circumstances to maintain the privacy of those who have inspired me.

The "Exhale" section includes interfaith prayers and poetry written by authors that speak to relief and happiness. Some of the works are from traditional scriptural sources (the Bible, Bhagavad Gita, and Qur'an, for example) and others are written by contemporary poets. Their uplifting words invite us to experience love, joy, and peace from many different perspectives.

Both sections offer "Breathing Light" meditations and questions for reflection as you accompany those you care for on this path. My greatest hope is that you will find this offering inspirational, comforting, and helpful, and that you will deepen into the compassionate presence that surrounds us all. —JH

About the Photography

Few of us take the time to pay close attention to the wonders that surround us in the natural world, to explore the essence of the flora, fauna and landscapes that we pass by. In the busyness and demands of our daily lives, we too often are cut off from the gifts of Creation either by being shut inside or by being so preoccupied with our thoughts, worries and responsibilities (and increasingly our cell phones and iPads) that we pass by things disconnected and unaware.

When we do stop and really see, we are amazed by the complexity of the textures, designs, structures and colors that we discover. When we look deeply at a flower or raindrops on a leaf or a waterfall, even for just a few moments, we can be transported to a different world—a world of beauty, of hope. We can be uplifted, connected to that which is eternal. We can breathe easier—exhaling the weight of things we are holding in, inhaling the Light that surrounds us—while being fully present to the wonders of nature.

The images shared in this book reflect moments in time when I was in the Presence in nature, when I was connected to that sense of wonder, when I experienced a few of the infinite miracles, small and large, that surround us within the natural world. I invite you to sit with them and let them draw you in. —DF

Inhale

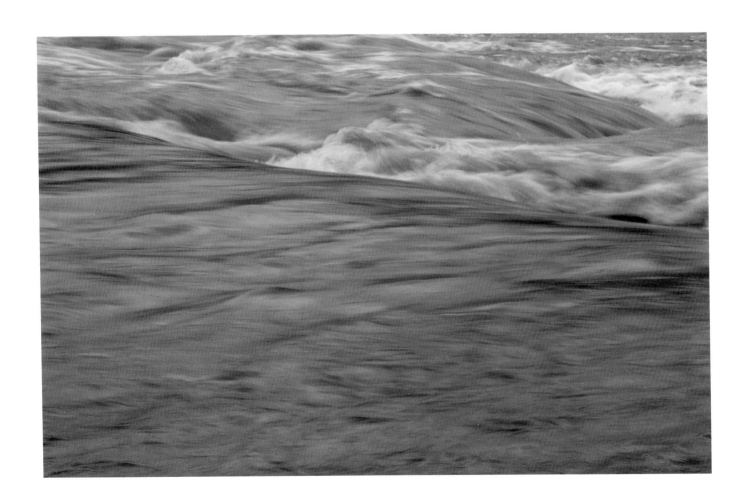

The Tiny Flame

Sometimes the light inside me feels like a tiny flame that could easily be extinguished if not protected. This small flame, residing deep in the core of my belly, flickers to remind me of its presence. It persists, even when surrounded by darkness, emptiness, nothingness.

Sitting in meditation I recognize my desire to grow the flame, to illuminate the darkness, to see what is present. I desire to fill my core, my belly, my entire body with light.

How do I grow this flame?

» By creating space through relaxation, calming my mind, relinquishing expectations, being present...

» By offering compassion for myself and others, recognizing that anyone at anytime can feel the fragility of their tiny flame...

» By sensing kindness from my body, my beloved, my friends, my canine companion...

» By embracing acts of love like wet dog kisses, holding my beloved's hand, exchanging greetings with neighbors, offering prayers, tending gardens, feeding birds, sharing a meal...

» By entering the Divine presence, basking in the light that radiates through me and connects me to all other light in the universe.

These are just a handful of the intentional practices I engage in to mindfully enter into the light.

Ah, my flame is now strong, brilliant, ever expanding. Simply thinking about these intentions has the desired effect. I realize that, no matter how tiny my flame feels, this light does not require protection—it can never be extinguished. This is the true Divine spark within me, within all of us. We are all Divine light. How will you grow your flame?

Breathing Light: Sit comfortably and find your breath, located in the center of your chest. Take several deep breaths, inhaling through your mouth and exhaling through your nose. As you inhale, imagine pulling faint light into your ribcage. Allow that light to expand and strengthen in your body until it is a bright fire. As you exhale, imagine breathing warm smiles onto those who most need them.

Seven Weeks

I've just met John, 93, and he is happy for the company. His first sentences require about an hour to communicate. I have a difficult time hearing his soft, garbled voice. He looks at me intently, struggling to express his thoughts. With effort, he announces, "Traffic, it's bad in Atlanta." This is his icebreaker, his topic of connection. I laugh. "Yes," I reply, "it certainly is." I reach out to hold his gnarled, shaking hand.

…

"Hi John, it's Julie," I exclaim. A broad smile crosses his face, "Hey Julie!" He recognizes me, and invites me to sit down. Today, his cognitive functions are fully engaged. We talk about baseball, engineering, and family. His memories are rich with anecdotes of past successes. I hold his hand, which is warm, steady, and certain. The hours pass quickly with much laughter.

…

I poke my head in the door to his room. He is sleeping soundly, snoring softly. I pull a chair up next to the bed. Sitting in silence, I form a light-filled connection. He wakens, looks at me, and smiles. His eyes search me for familiarity, recognition. None register, but he continues smiling. I introduce myself, take his hand, and begin again.

…

As I walk down the hall, here he comes. Wheeled about by a hospice coworker, waving his arms. He greets everyone he meets with a booming "Hello." He is so happy his entire body is smiling. I walk over to him, saying "Hi John, it's Julie!" "So good to see you," he shouts. My colleague says, "He is having a great day." I lean down, take his hand, and wish him well.

…

Unable to feed himself, I offer to help. Surveying the food, I joke, "Shall we start with dessert?" "Sure," he says, "And sweet tea, please." I dish up small bits of ice cream, waiting for him to swallow. His reflexes are very slow, turtle speed. When he finishes, I reach over and take his hand. He raises my hand to his lips and kisses the back of it. "Thank you," he says. I am moved to tears.

…

I knock on his door and he flinches. "Hi John, it's Julie," I say with a big smile. He searches my face but nothing registers. I ask him if he'd like company and he says yes. He jerks again and peers at the empty space beside him. "What is it?" I ask. "It's Melvin, my dog," he responds. "Oh, tell me about Melvin," I invite. Melvin is a dachshund, overweight, and very spunky.

…

The room is cool enough that I need a sweater. His body is weak, a remnant of skin and bones. Eyes half open, body trembling, death is near. I offer him water, holding a half-filled syringe to his lips. He drinks it in, and indicates that he wants more. We continue like this for some time. I take his hand, his left eye fixes on my face. I smile and let him know how happy I am to be with him.

❖

God Is With You

Go, for God sends you.
Be strong and of good courage,
do not fear or be saddened,
for God is with you
wherever you go.

At your right is the angel Michael.
At your left is the angel Gabriel.
In front of you is the angel Uriel.
Behind you is the angel Raphael.
And above you is
the divine presence of God.

God will guard your soul,
coming and going, now and forever.
God will bless you, keep you,
and be gracious to you.
God will gaze upon you,
and give you peace.

Breathing Light: Inhale, "May I feel God's presence." Exhale, "May God give you peace." How do you feel God?

River of Light

Often, I envision the Beloved as an all-encompassing collective light energy from which everything emerges. All that is born into existence comes from, and is part of, God's transcendent and immanent life force, what I refer to as the "River of Light." Galaxies, stars, planets, humans, plants, animals, minerals, and inanimate objects are infused with this *élan vital*. The same light that radiates through me radiates through you, and through everything else.

I like to visualize the River of Light as a enormous waterway filled with animated light particles having no beginning and no end—a continuous stream of glistening sparkles, similar to the light reflecting off the colorful glitter of snow. I imagine that upon death, my personal light particles, released from my body, mind, and soul, will be absorbed back into the universal energetic life flow. My light will mingle with the River of Light, and revel in the union. Then perhaps, after a respite of undetermined time, "my" light will be cycled back into the cosmos in whatever form creation requires at that particular moment, as a single being, or perhaps dispersed over many elements.

I've experienced the Beloved as a River of Light on various occasions. One particular story involves Jacque, a teacher and mentor of mine who died on Christmas Eve a decade ago.

With a physical likeness to the Laughing Buddha, Jacque was mischievous, fun, and always smiling. She was an ordained Methodist minister, a therapist, an intuitive psychic, and a wisdom teacher. Having studied many religious traditions, healing arts, and psychotherapy modalities, Jacque wove together the insights she accumulated during her sixty years on the planet into a three-year educational intensive program for people like me. The training was an early expression of interfaith chaplaincy, and her mission was to teach us how to be a healing presence to all beings, everywhere.

Jacque was diagnosed with her third round of breast cancer half way through our program. She willingly underwent the chemo, radiation, and other treatments recommended by her oncologist. She also learned Qigong so that she could more easily tune into her *chi*, made use of the healing powers of herbs, crystals, and intercessory prayer, and held hands-on healing ceremonies to bless her body. Jacque's life force and zest for living was strong. Although her prognosis was bleak, she lived another three years.

While in hospice, and shortly before her death, Jacque requested that her friends and students hold a three-day vigil upon her passing. A three-day vigil is very important for those who believe that upon death the soul leaves the earthly body immediately but then hovers around it for three days. During these 72 hours, the soul may decide

to reunite with the body causing an instance of miraculous resurrection. In such an atmosphere of bereavement and eternal hope, friends and family hold a vigil. Participants chant religious texts, meditate, ring bells, read poetry aloud, beat drums, or share other prayerful expressions. Since there were many of us who wanted to participate in this vigil, we knew we could grant Jacque's request and honor the 72-hour tradition. Nancy, a longtime friend, hosted the vigil.

On the first evening of the vigil, I arrived at Nancy's house around 6:00 pm. A three-season indoor porch had been arranged as the gathering space, and a group of friends had been there most of the day reading poetry, sharing stories about Jacque, and meditating. Shortly after I joined them, the group dispersed to get something to eat. Since I had not participated in a vigil before, I presumed that at least one person should be in the room at all times to be present for Jacque. Rather than joining the others in the kitchen, I remained. With the room to myself I stood and began to chant spiritual mantras and sing musical praise to Jacque.

After what seemed to be just a few minutes, I sat down and meditated. I began my contemplative practice by closing my eyes, centering myself, tuning into my breath, and calming my thoughts. When I felt peaceful and open, I reached out mentally to Jacque and asked her where she was. Immediately, an image emerged in my mind's eye of an egg dropping into a fallopian tube. I laughed aloud with delight. It appeared that some part of Jacque's energy was preparing to participate once again in the universal life cycle. I became distracted for a moment wondering where and when she might take form, and if I could find her. I wondered if this message was the point of my sitting vigil. Fortunately, my longing to embrace Jacque one more time drew me deeper into my heart and the meditation.

I next asked Jacque if there was anything she wanted to share with me about the place she had passed over to. Again in my mind's eye, an image of a very dark space materialized. A large door began to open slowly toward me letting in a small, brilliant shaft of light. Instantaneously I felt my heart open and intense compassion wash over my body. The door opened a bit further and I saw the vast River of Light. I sensed a strong desire to move toward it, and had awareness that my body, mind, and soul—all of my energy particles—were being called home. It is difficult for me to describe the insight I had as I was drawn toward the light. Words such as unconditional love, union, oneness, and God come close, but the impression is one of an easy willingness to leave life as I knew it to enter the light.

I mentally moved closer to the light until I was a few feet away. Suddenly the door slammed closed and I was left in the dark space, realizing that the communication with Jacque was complete. I sat for a few moments allowing the imagery to sink in and expressing prayerful gratitude for Jacque's messages. I concluded the meditation, opened my eyes, and realized that everyone else was still in the kitchen. My sense was that I had been at Nancy's about twenty minutes or so, and it was probably time to be heading home.

I opened the kitchen door to check the clock. It was 8:00 p.m. Two hours had passed. I asked Nancy if her clock was correct, and she responded yes, that I had been chanting and meditating for two hours. She said they had all remained in the kitchen because no one had wanted to disturb "my sacred energy connection with Jacque." Several of them had felt her presence, too. I headed home in awe.

Breathing Light: Find a place outside where you can sit comfortably, preferably in nature. Situate yourself facing the sun. As you inhale, imagine a river of light flowing into the front of your body. As you exhale, imagine the same river of light flowing out of you and reaching anyone who is in need of light—past, present, or future. After a few minutes, give thanks to the sun.

Ninety-Two

Determined, parched lips
Pursed, opened, then pursed again
Mind probing gaps for phrases
Seeking the thought present a moment ago
Different words stumble and fall

Brow furrows under a cloud of white
Eyes stare at transcendent emptiness
Trying, once more, surveying…nothing

Bewildered frustration melts
A smile crosses her face
She looks at me directly, intently
"Oh well" she says, "I'm 92.
Whatcha gonna do?"

Released

She lies in bed under a mound of covers, her dark, curly hair slightly tamed by a colorful scarf, her face peaceful despite the intubation tube. I slip my hand under the edge of the blanket to find hers swollen and slightly cool. Wrapping my fingers around her hand, I tell her, "I am going to sit with you and hold you in the Light." Even though she is in a coma, I invite her to let me know if she needs anything.

In my mind's eye, a portal opens, emitting light in particles that begin to form a tunnel. They twinkle brilliantly, like newly fallen snow sparkles in the sunlight. Its entryway pulses, beckoning. The light is a spectacular vision, energetic, beautiful, and welcoming.

I take several deep breaths drinking in the scene. My awareness shifts to her hand in mine. I squeeze it slightly to remind her I am here. A small, human

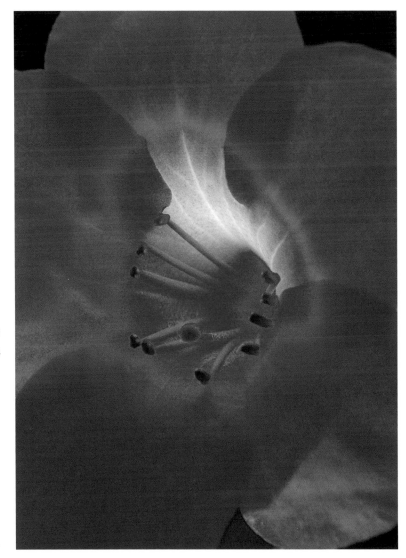

form appears in the tunnel of light, clearly past the halfway point. I sense this is she, headed into the portal surrounded by clouds of light particles. There is a strong pull, a willing force, emanating from this small figure, moving further into the tunnel, but also, there is something holding her back. I look to see if there are any threads of attachment connected to the figure and indeed there is a single thread still waiting to be cut.

In my mind's ear, she says clearly, "Release my body from this machine." I am startled by this message. I gently squeeze her unresponsive hand again, and ask her if she has a message for me. She states again unambiguously and more loudly, "Release my body."

I see the image again of the small figure straining against the hold of the last thread. She wishes to complete her passage. The thread is tied directly to her request. It is the ventilator keeping her alive. She doesn't want this, and I sense she is asking me to deliver that message. I leave her to find the nurse, to relay her wish.

As I depart the hospice unit, I mentally reach out and wish her safe travels.

Breathing Light: Sit comfortably with your eyes closed. Place your attention on your breath and notice your chest rising and falling. Imagine a tunnel of light that could help those you love transition over to death. Observe the texture, brilliance, resonance, and other qualities of this light. Give thanks for the mystery of it all.

Gatekeeper

The heart is a gatekeeper of death.

To accept loss, the heart recognizes
what no longer works,
what has come to pass,
what is asking to die in us.

It is a sacred dance, entering the heart,
a time of transition,
a sense of impermanence,
an indication of change.

This ephemeral dance illuminates
that which we resist and
that which we embrace,
that which causes pain and
that which brings us joy,
that which we discard and
that for which we yearn.

It enters us into the flow
of comprehending choices,
of birthing desires,
of craving permanence.

Embraced by the heart, death is an invitation
to celebrate each moment,
to respond to the fullness of life,
to appreciate omnipresent gifts.

Death is a gatekeeper of the heart.

The Saints in Our Corners

My parents were Catholic, and I was raised in this tradition. Every Sunday, from the time I was born until I turned 18, I went to mass. When I was young, we attended a large New York cathedral, which I recall being cold, dark, and damp. The mass was said in Latin, so I understood none of it, but I loved observing the older

women in their white gloves and head coverings saying the rosary.

I, too, had a rosary made of small faux pearls on a gold chain with a beautiful cross. I prayed the rosary in church, hoping that both the Blessed Virgin Mary and God would answer my requests to safeguard my relatives, friends, and animals. The rosary could be confusing—so much suffering to address and so many Mysteries to meditate on. The Joyful, Glorious, and Luminous were easier to think about than the Sorrowful with their attendant agony, thorns, torment, and crucifixion—all too much for a small child to manage. I mostly focused on reciting Hail Mary and Our Father prayers as I moved my little fingers across the beads.

The rosary contained a tiny metal figure of Jesus stretched over the metal cross. Each time I prayed, I was reminded of his crucifixion. It was painful to look at the cross and remember the priests and nuns in Sunday school telling me that Jesus did this for me. I could not grasp why Jesus would think I wanted him to suffer, no less die. I often wished he had asked me what I really wanted so that we might have cleared up such a horrible misunderstanding.

What I remember most about being in the cathedral was my mother telling me to stop swinging my feet in the pew and to sit still. The booming voice of the priest, the bowed heads, and the ritual of communion all seemed so mystical. My favorite part was entering the small vestibule where the tiny candles were lit, putting a nickel in the metal donation box, and then saying a prayer and lighting my own candle. I was certain that this ritual was magical, and that whatever prayer I said would come true. Mostly I prayed for the healing of others. I would stare up at the statue of the particular saint watching over this collection of prayers and flames and look for a flicker of response, some sort of acknowledgment that my prayer had been understood. I was never quite sure whether they moved or heard me, but I was willing to spend a nickel each Sunday and imagine that the saints were in my corner ready to intercede in answer to my prayers.

These days, I sit with people who are nearing the end of their lives, holding them in the Beloved's Light, a special form of prayer. Although my prayer beads are no longer the rosary, and the angels and saints who offer aid appear in a different form, my desire for healing and wholeness of all beings persists. I am certain, also, that Jesus understands my wish to end suffering and that he guides me each step of the way in this quest. My gratitude for compassionate wisdom is endless.

❖

Breathing Light: With journal in hand, find a peaceful place to rest. Close your eyes and imagine yourself as a small child. Allow an image to emerge of a time when you experienced the mystical. Breathe deeply and invite your whole self to feel and reflect upon the encounter. If moved to do so, write about how this experience may still influence you.

Unbearable

"If you can survive it,"
she says,
"then it's not really
unbearable."

A response of
"not so"
arises deep
from within my bones.

I remember
unbearable.

Psychic pain
so crisp and vibrant
that my nerves
threatened
to ignite extinction.

Physical agony
from separation
after being held together
for years,
connection evaporating
into desolation.

Grief
accompanied by
so many tears
that my skin

began to burn,
a torrent of scouring
inside and out.

Heartache
and torment
conjoining
to rend my body
in half
and fracture my soul.

A complete
and utterly agonizing
dissolution into
the void.

Yes, I remember
unbearable.

A heart
broken open,
the intolerable pain
transforming
into excruciating
unconditional love.

Unchained energy
discharging
from body, mind,
and spirit,

broadcasting
radiant life force.

Light
illuminating
the intersection
of transcendence
and immanence,
detection
of a collective we.

Awareness
of suffering so acute and
steadfast love so exquisite,
that compassion
was the solitary
sane response.

A complete
and utterly fervent
dissolution into
becoming.

Thriving emerging
from surviving.

Yes, I remember
unbearable.

A Tribute
to Maya
(November 4, 2010)

My beloved canine companion Maya transitioned yesterday morning. My heart is filled with both sadness of her loss and immense gratitude for the two years we had together.

I adopted Maya in June 2008 from a woman who had rescued her from the pound and was fostering her. No one was quite sure how old she was at that time—our best guess was between 9 and 11 years. Maya was a Norwegian Elkhound / Husky hybrid. Originally from Norway (or so her ancestry suggests), it is not clear how she found her way to Southwest Michigan nine years ago. Her breed attended to corralling elk, wolves, and bears. She must have performed her work very well since these predators have not been spotted in the area for several decades!

About four weeks ago Maya was diagnosed with hemangiosarcoma, cancer of the spleen, an incurable and aggressive disease. Over these last few weeks we did our best to keep her comfortable with medications but her pain did not abate and she continued to deteriorate. Yesterday she was euthanized and seemed to pass peacefully to join other precious spirits.

Maya and I saved each other. I learned so much from her in these two years. She taught me about unconditional love, expressing joy with wild abandon, and asking for what you need. Maya taught me about boundaries, self-protection, and sounding off when appropriate. A furry ball of sweetness and love, she could also exhibit a warrior's fierceness, attributes we all need.

Maya will be remembered for her joyous energy, smiling face, and unending stream of kisses. She elicited joy from people everywhere we went. Maya shared herself fully and in such a way that we all learned more about ourselves in her presence. She was full of surprises but could also bring peace, and tranquility. She loved her human pack, and could often be found lying under my desk with her paw forming the connection between us. I feel her absence acutely and miss her very much.

Breathing Light: Sit comfortably, inhaling through your nose and exhaling through your mouth. Following this pattern, take several deep breaths, placing your attention in your heart. Imagine holding the hand or paw of a loved one who is now deceased. Visualize their presence with you and share with them something that they would find joyful.

Gifts

During a recent chaplaincy visit to the local hospital, I met with three patients awaiting organ transplants. Each bestowed upon me unique gifts that deepened my sense of the awe and impermanence of life.

The first patient gave me the gifts of serenity and connection. He was scheduled for his third round of an intensive, weeklong chemotherapy. He knew the effect this poison would have on his body, but he was also up for it. He said, "It is in God's hands." His calm attitude was remarkable to witness, and his sense of peace palpable. When we prayed together for intercessory healing, he wrapped his bare hands around my gloved hands and held on tightly. I was immediately self-conscious about the gloves, a barrier between us, but soon shifted to a sense of serenity because of the strength of his person.

The second patient shared with me the gifts of curiosity and joy. He and his wife delighted in discovering that I was a Quaker and were interested in learning about this tradition. We talked about theology, conscientious objectors during the Vietnam War, Richard Nixon (a self-proclaimed Quaker), and oatmeal. They wanted to understand the differences between Quakers and Presbyterians and Baptists, their respective traditions. They quizzed me until they understood a few theological differences, but also admitted "there are hardly any at all."

This patient had a kidney transplant a couple of years ago. He was now feeling awful and the doctors had yet to determine what was wrong. Both he and his wife stated that it was "in God's hands," but that they also hoped that God would give the doctors the wisdom they needed to diagnose the issue. We prayed together for wisdom and healing.

The third patient offered the gifts of kindness and humility. Her first bone marrow transplant (BMT) had not succeeded so she was here for a second try. The regimen, as she described it, sounded grueling. She said she only had a 40% chance of the BMT working, and then if it did stick, a mere 40% chance of surviving after that. She mentioned a number of times that it was "in God's hands" whether she lived or died. What was hardest for her was leaving her meaningful work as a pediatrician and not knowing if she would ever get back to it. This saddened her greatly.

Her spirits lifted as she told me about how important chaplains are in a hospital setting. She shared several stories ending each with "I could not have done this without a chaplain being present." She implored me to understand and trust "how valuable you are—don't let any anyone tell you differently." We prayed together for healing. When I was finished with my part, she jumped in and continued to pray for me, "an angel sent to help me heal." I was deeply moved and humbled by her kind words.

These patients referred to their conditions as being, "in God's hands." The looks in their eyes and the sincerity in their voices expressed the vulnerability of the human condition and a wish for peace. They feared the potency of the treatments, knowing that they would pull through the procedure or that they would die. They were firm in their faith—it was in God's hands and they found solace in this.

I felt the presence of God flowing through them and me, meeting somewhere in the middle and encompassing us together, completely. God was touching their hurting bodies, minds, and hearts with compassion and mercy. The experience of sitting with these patients gave new meaning to the words, "For where two or three gather in my name, there am I with them"(Matthew 18:20). I felt a deep connection—to the patient, to God, all of us linked through the wonder of suffering, hope, and grace.

As I now reflect on these connections, I find a practical and a mystical aspect in each of them. The practical in visits, conversation, and prayer; the mystical in an ever-revealing God surrounding and infiltrating all. Each time I have such intimate encounters, it is life-changing. I have been cracked open yet again, moved more deeply into awe, and have come face to face with the unconditional love and the compassionate presence of God.

❖

Breathing Light: Relax your body and rest in a comfortable position. Next, relax your thoughts. You might even massage your forehead or temples to aid the relaxation of your mind. Allow your thoughts to meander gently back through the past 24 hours surveying gifts both given and received. Inhale gratitude into your heart; exhale joy for all.

Tranquility

Soft as a cloud
Still as a pond
She lies there
Her gentle breath
Lapping against the edge
Of waters
Seeking to transport her
While she dreams
Continuously
And recedes
Into liberation
And serenity

❖

Forsaken

Searching my face through liquid eyes, she cries out, "Why has God forsaken me?"

What can I offer such a desperate plea? No response will be adequate to meet this place of suffering.

"May I hold your hand," I reply. An affirmative nod allows space for us to join in physical connection. I can sense her body relaxing.

"I'm so sorry you are feeling alone today," I say with gentleness. The eyes fill with tears once again and they begin to spill down her cheeks. In this mental darkness of delirium, where no light can penetrate, the stroke of a hand reaches through and touches the heart. She takes a deep, laboring breath. In our stillness, she implores quietly, "Why has God forsaken me?" I hold her hand, honoring her experience, while I feel God's presence surrounding us like a thick, warm cloak. I allow my words to come slowly.

"I believe that God is a compassionate God who suffers with us. God is here, right now, and feels your pain deeply. You are not alone. I am holding you in my heart." I squeeze her hand.

She searches my face again, closes her eyes, and leans back resting her head as if to lay down a heavy burden. She whispers, "Why has God forsaken me?"

I squeeze her hand. In our silence I remember, "Be still and know that I am God."

Psalms of Compassion

Dearly Beloved, you begin each morning showering me with your unconditional love; I rejoice and am glad all of my days. Help me to embrace your love as my first light today and always.

I look to thee, my Beloved, to give me bounty in due season. When you give to me, I gather it up; when you open your hand, I am filled with good things. When I cannot find you, I miss you; when I die, I will return to dust and renew the majestic ground with my spirit. Help me to receive your bounty, delight in your majesty, and offer my own bounty to others.

How precious is your unconditional love, my Beloved, in the shadow of your wings we find a sanctuary. I feast abundantly and drink from the river of your delights. You are the fountain of life; in your light, do I find light. Help me to express the light that resides in me with the world.

When I am afraid, I put my trust in you, my Beloved, trusting without fear. You know everything, and in that understanding I find strength to handle anything that comes. Help me to lean on you when faced with a difficult situation, and to know deep in my bones that your love is ever present.

Yea, you are my rock and my fortress; dearly Beloved, lead me and guide me safely into everything that life requires of me, for you are my refuge. Into your hand I commit my spirit; your faithful guidance has restored me. Help me to recognize and follow your guidance in each moment.

Only for you, my Beloved, do I wait; for I know it is you, the one who bestows all blessings, who will answer and provide what I need. Help me to receive your many gifts in the blessings you present me.

You show me the path of life, my Beloved; in your presence there is fullness of joy, expansion of spirit, and relief of difficulties. Your hands bestow blessings for evermore. Help me to comprehend the expansive nature of all that I am.

Yes, you light the lamp of all existence; my Beloved, you lighten my darkness. You, who need no light, are all light. Help me comprehend your vast reach, touching all of existence, and nurture the light-filled lamp within us all.

Guard my life, my Beloved, for I am under your care; I trust in you to help me. You are my guardian; care for me as I cry out in need. Gladden my soul, for to you do I offer up all of my burdens. Help me to feel your presence guarding and holding me, particularly in times of distress.

I bless you, my Beloved, for the counsel you provide; in the night, you instruct me through my heart. I keep you always before me; because having you near me provides refuge. Therefore my heart is glad, and my soul rejoices; my body also feels secure. Help me to trust that, through your refuge, all is well and my needs will be satisfied.

In peace I will both lie down and sleep; for you alone, my Beloved, assure that all is well and safe and good. Help me to relax and find peace within my body, mind, and soul.

Amen

When Death
Is Near

"This is my grandmother, Charlotte," Jane says as she inclines her head toward the elderly woman lying in the bed. "She is almost 100 years old and lived on her own until just a few weeks ago when she collapsed. How close is death?"

I gaze at Charlotte, a beautiful woman whose peaceful smile indicates a physiological contentment. Her calm breathing is interrupted episodically by rattling, coughing sounds. She has been sleeping the past five days with periodic consciousness and movement in her limbs and has not taken in any food. I look at her granddaughter and say with compassion, "No one knows for sure, but I think death is near."

There are particular signs that appear at the end of life, indications that the body is beginning to wind down. Each human is unique, so not everyone experiences these symptoms. Some people move rapidly through the stages of slowing down, while others can take years, cycling back into life with bursts of energy.

Toward the last few weeks of life, a dying person may begin to face confusion about where they are, what day it is, or who is visiting with them. Some hold this disorientation lightly and with a sense of humor while others are frightened by it. Hallucinations may occur, intensifying the state of uncertainty. Physically, the body begins to change. Heart rate, blood pressure, skin color, breathing, and temperature all shift to accommodate the dying process.

In the final days or hours, a dying person may spend most of his or her time sleeping, although waves of energy and restlessness can occur, too. Eating and drinking become less appealing, and it may be difficult for the person to swallow. Blood pressure tends to drop further, as does the heart rate, and breathing slows. Sometimes the mouth will remain open and the eyelids will not close all the way. Eventually as death draws near, the person will cease breathing and become unresponsive. Pupils will not react to light, and there may be a loss of bowel and bladder control.

People who are declining may begin to talk about "going home" or visiting loved ones who have died before them, including animal companions. Many of my hospice patients have said that they are looking forward to reuniting with their spouse, friends, siblings, and/or pets. Sometimes, they will see these loved ones in their presence and talk to the visitors as if the dead were in the room. I love hearing these conversations and often join in as though we were all having tea together.

Jane leans over and kisses her grandmother's forehead. I witness the love they shared for half a century. I say gently, "Even when you are prepared for it, death can feel like a shock. You may wish to think about how you would like to honor your grandmother at her time of death. In the meantime, talk to her, hold her hand, and let her know you are here. She will feel your love."

Breathing Light: In a quiet place, remember a loved one who has died. Have a conversation with your loved one as though he or she were with you now. What would you like to share about yourself? How would you like to express your love? When you are finished, offer gratitude for your loved one's presence in your life.

Carolyn

Wee hours of dawn
Crickets are sleeping
Peace fills the damp air

Nightlight casts shadows
Surveying the room
Calm about the place

Breathing is restful
Labored effort gone
Chest inhale, exhale

Slight smile on face
Eyes twitching in dream
A leg jumps, then still

Early to begin
Late to fall asleep
Body exhausted

Sit with love and grace
Holding Carolyn
In the Light of God

It began sometime ago, I guess.
I'm not really sure how it started…

It was manageable but has now escalated.
I'm uncertain about what to do, or how to be…

It came on suddenly, out of the blue.
I didn't know what hit me, or why . . .

It was imperceptible at first, the probability slight.
I thought the odds were with me . . .

The New Normal

It continues to spread, intensify, worsen.
I learn to cope and then it changes . . .

It was always a possibility, lingering in the background.
I never gave credence to it materializing . . .

It returned, again, this time to stay.
I had hoped I was finished . . .

. . . this, now, is my new normal.

Acceptance and patience in not-knowing.
Courage and strength in bearing witness.
Love and compassion in all actions.

Good Hands

Gloved and gowned, I enter Mr. Baxter's room and stand at the foot of his bed. Closing my eyes, I listen to the rhythm of the ventilator, perfectly synchronized in time, like a metronome, that supports his breathing. Its artificial nature is both disturbing and miraculous, the paradox required to keep this man alive. His body is swollen from head to toe and radiating heat. I was told he is in a coma and unresponsive. Still, I introduce myself and announce that I am happy to be here visiting with him. I reach for an armchair, pull it up to the side of the bed, and sit down, all while describing my actions to him. I never know how much a patient in this condition can hear or understand, so I tend to articulate what I am doing as I would with any patient whose awareness is fully present.

Seated beside him, I close my eyes, steady my mind, and place my attention in my heart. Over the next few minutes, my breathing regulates, my heart rate slows, and a sense of calmness, light, and peace fills my body. I am now prepared to prayerfully hold Mr. Baxter in the Light.

In Quakerism (The Religious Society of Friends), Light plays a key role in prayer and healing. Within this tradition, we hold someone in the Light and ask for God's presence to illumine a person, situation, or problem, whether in concern or thanksgiving. We often do this by first connecting to our own inner power and inspiration

of the Beloved (God, Christ, the Holy Spirit). This reveals to us our true motivations, guides us with wisdom, and gives us strength to act on this guidance—thus bringing us into unity with the Spirit. Often, when I am holding someone in the Light, I imagine them surrounded by love-filled aura that permeates every part of their being. This luminosity is sourced by all beings, so it is best if I am centered and calm.

As I sit next to Mr. Baxter, I am aware that his body is twitching about every three or four seconds, seemingly random nerve impulses firing and contracting his muscles as he otherwise lies still. I receive a spiritual nudge to take his hand but I am hesitant. I don't want my gloved hand to be the sensation that connects to his skin. It seems too sterile and impersonal. Yet, I am also aware of the precautions and do not want to remove my glove for his protection and mine. I sit a few more minutes and then receive another nudge.

This time, I place a sheet over his hand, and then put my hand on top of his. I instantly feel a physical and energetic connection with Mr. Baxter, and intuitively begin to gently rub the back of his hand. Immediately, he stops twitching. I continue moving my hand slowly over the surface of his sheet-covered hand and he remains still. I detect a relaxation within his body that begins to deepen into a greater stillness. It is as if his entire body is sighing, letting down, and relaxing.

I wonder how this can be after witnessing the constant, involuntary twitching. Is it possible that simple touch, just rubbing the back of a hand, would allow a body in such discomfort to relax? What are the sensory receptors telling the muscles, or nerve endings, or whatever is prompting the contracting? Is my touch reassuring him that he is not alone? Is there a cognitive function that recognizes this connection? Does this physical contact register as healing presence? Regardless, I feel immense gratitude for whatever I am able to offer Mr. Baxter, continue to stroke his hand for about twenty minutes, and hold him in the healing Light.

When I open my eyes, I look up at his face. About three feet above the head of his bed, I "see" four spiritual beings floating in the air. They look like pencil outline drawings of angels—wispy and shimmery, rather than solid and filled in. They register for me as Mr. Baxter's guardian angels, cloud of witnesses, or spirit guides. The beings are waiting patiently, ready to collect Mr. Baxter up in their arms upon his death. I reach out mentally to Mr. Baxter and ask him if he is ready to go. I hear a clear "no" and can feel that his life force is still very strong. The angels seem to sense this too. They appear to be in no hurry, with no agenda—only a state of relaxed readiness. I let Mr. Baxter know that they are here.

I continue to sit and pray, holding Mr. Baxter in the Light and watching the angels float. I realize that it is likely Mr. Baxter will die by the time I return to the hospice unit. I am at peace in sensing that he will also be in good hands when he transitions.

Haiku Journey

fourth round of cancer
chemo and radiation
hardly worth effort

in numberless ways
grief penetratingly present
struggle breathes calm light

end is close at hand
dense cool air seeks to envelope
until we meet again

union unfolds birth
love hunts for connection
death remembers we

Radiant Lamps

Sufism speaks about the Beloved as the Sun, the center of everything, the source of all light burning brightly and feeding life. The Ninety-Nine Names of God, or the attributes of the Beloved within the Qur'an, such as Mercy, Compassion, Love, and Peace, are the rays of light emanating from the sun. As these rays of light touch the stars, the earth, human beings, and other life forms, all are infused with light and the aspects of God. The entire world, and all its parts, become signs of the existence of the Beloved. We are engaged with this light-filled actuality every day. Simply to live, therefore, is to sense the Beloved's presence in everything and everyone.

Sufis describe how the Beloved resides within us as light. Within each of us is a lamp containing a brightly burning light, the illumination of the Beloved. Throughout the trials of childhood, we have learned fear and built defenses. This causes our lamps to become covered with dust, with soot. Regular prayer is a way of polishing our lamp. Meditating is like pulling out a dust rag and removing the layers of grime that cover our lamp. As we continue to polish our lamp a little each day, we reveal our light to others. The light that radiates from our lamp is a healing presence for the world.

Breathing Light: Center yourself, locate your breath, and place your attention in your heart. Inhale and exhale through your mouth, slowly and with intention. After a few moments, imagine yourself as the pure light of compassion and love. As you inhale, allow this pure compassion and love to permeate your entire being. As you exhale, send it to anyone who is suffering.

On Solid Ground

As the lightning bolts begin to split the night air, I realize that I am standing in the middle of a prairie field. Surrounded by darkness as black as coal, I can just make out the wood's edge during the flashes of light. The dense forest is a potential place of refuge compared to the open grassland, but I stay put, continuing to yell in anguish at the sky, at God, at the universe. My heart is so fractured, I don't care about the danger that makes me jump each time a jolt of electric-

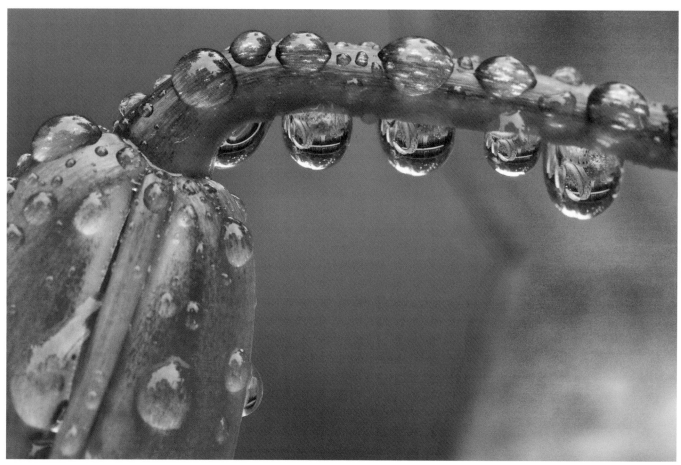

ity is let loose. I dare God to take me out, do me in, drop me in my tracks. I welcome an end to the unbearable psychic and embodied pain threatening to rend me in half.

A thunderous clap is the only response I hear. My anger increases and I curse with despairing rage in the direction of the boom. After losing so much over the past year that defined me—my home, my work, my relationship, my identity—I discovered today that my treasured canine companion has cancer with only a few weeks to live. How could God, the Beloved, let this happen? How could God not see my fragility, or comprehend my need for uncomplicated love, or answer my prayers of safekeeping for all beings? Why…why now… why at all? My dog has been my bedrock, my best friend, my confidant, and my teacher. We have had thirteen years together beginning with the day he mysteriously appeared on my back porch at only six weeks old. He has seen me through all of the wrenching choices, the letting go…through picking up the pieces and moving forward. My grief over this impending new loss is so intense that I doubt I have the reserves to survive it. I fall to the ground sobbing, unable to care about whether I live or die. I beg God to release me from my sorrow.

The clouds open and warm rain begins to pour in drops so big and heavy that they make indentations in the sandy soil. My clothes are getting soaked. I close my eyes as the water washes over me in sheets. The drenching liquid penetrates my anger, my pain, my suffering and relaxes their hardness. My tension begins to ease, and I am aware that the earth is embracing me closely, supporting my strained body. Nature is comforting me, rinsing me clean of my anguish, fears, and loss, while wrapping her sandy, grassy arms around me.

Over time, I begin to feel the Beloved's presence everywhere. It dawns on me . . . God has been here the entire time, holding me intimately like a cherished child, suffering with my suffering, and bestowing compassion through the elements of earth and water.

Sinking into this sacred space, this spot of land, I allow the impending death of my heart mate to register fully. I open to the incredible pain and grant the rain permission to bathe and soothe my grief. I am losing a precious loved one, as so many before me have experienced, and so many after me will, too. Exposed to the oneness of suffering, I feel the bittersweet grief that can only come from such a deep reservoir of love. Bereavement is part of the human condition, and this binds me to all those experiencing penetrating sorrow. On solid ground, I say a prayer for all of us, resurrect my body, and head for home to be with the one I adore in his final days.

Breathing Light: Sit comfortably, close your eyes, and find your breath. Take several deliberate breaths, inhaling and exhaling deeply. Open your heart to someone you love that is suffering. As you inhale, take in their pain. As you exhale, send them happiness, relief, and love. After a few minutes, move your body gently, open your eyes, and orient yourself to your surroundings. Express gratitude for your loved one and yourself.

Everything Changes, Even Grief

I was told that
even when one is expecting death,
when the mind prepares for it,
death still comes as a shock.
So true.

A finality sets in that was not present,
until the ultimate moment.
The last breath, the passing over,
the ending, the final transition.
I cannot get the person back.
Their physicality is gone forever.
A jolt and blow of disbelief.

Density commences,
a raw numbness,
a congealing of sorts,
like an opaque fog.
At the same time
an unlocking of ultimate clarity
reveals what is real.

Priorities line up
in a pyramid formation—
love at the top, or is it at the bottom
as the formation that supports everything else.
Pain and sadness set in,
grief expressing itself
through the body's responses—
tears, walking in circles, numbness.

An acute awareness
of all that is living—
birds chirping, dogs barking,
people laughing,
trees shimmering in the breeze.

My inner light feels cloaked,
protected by a heavy cape
someone or something
has wrapped around me.

My heart aches for
and celebrates
impermanence,
the cycle of life and death,
that everything changes, even grief.

I cannot remember
how to turn on the oven timer,
nor what I walked into the bedroom for,
nor what day it is.
Such is the affect of loss.
But this, too, shall pass.

Breathing Light: May all beings find their way through grief.

Exhale

I Am in All Hearts

—The Bhavagad Gita

I am where all things began,
The issuing forth of all creatures,
Known to the wise in their love
When they worship with hearts overflowing.
The light that lives in the sun,
Lighting all the world,
The light of the moon,
The light that is in fire;
Know that light to be mine.

My energy enters the earth,
Sustaining all that lives.
I become the moon,
Giver of water and sap,
To feed the plants and the trees.
Flame of life in all,
I consume the many foods,
Turning them into strength
That upholds the body.
I am in all hearts.

The Gathering

—Becca Holohan

We are loved by an unending love, ahavat olam,
sings my aunt as she waters her plants.
Her gold bracelets jingle as droplets feed
thirsty leaves reaching for light,
for the sustenance in her hands.
The sun and moon rise and fade,
autumn frosts the windows as the women
gather.

We are loved by an unending love, ahavat olam,
sings my grandmother as she kneads bread
for the new moon gathering, paints hamsas
on the door to protect all who enter from
harm. The women arrive in twos and threes,
warm bursts of laughter and knowing winks,
curly hair wild at their shoulders.

We are loved by an unending love, ahavat olam,
they chant together, dancing, arms wrapped
around each other, the scent of my
grandmother's bread
filling the house, breath and song and
heartbeats rising,
weaving magic, weaving hope.

❖

Breathing Light: May all beings be
loved by an unending love.

Light of All Souls

—*Hazrat Inayat Khan*

O Thou the light of all souls,
the life of all beings,
the healer of hearts,
all sufficient and all powerful God,
the forgiver of our shortcomings,
free us from all pain and suffering
and make us Thy instruments
that we may in our turn
free others from pain and suffering
and that we may impart to them
Thy light, Thy life, Thy joy and Thy peace.

Amen

Every Moment of Your Goodness

—Traditional Buddhist Healing Prayer

Just as the soft rains fill the streams,
pour into the rivers, and join together
in the oceans, so may the power of every moment
of your goodness flow forth and heal all beings,
those here now, those gone before, those yet to
come.

By the power of every moment of your goodness
may your heart's wishes soon be fulfilled
as completely shining as the bright full moon,
as magically as by a wish-fulfilling gem.

By the power of every moment of your goodness,
may all dangers be averted and all disease be gone.
May no obstacle come across your way.
May you enjoy fulfillment and long life.

❖

Breathing Light: Inhale, "Goodness fills my heart." Exhale, "May my goodness flow to all beings." What helps you remember the power of your goodness?

Search Me and Know Me
(Psalm 139)

My Beloved, you have searched me and known me!
You know when I sit down and when I rise up;
you discern my thoughts from afar.
You search out my path and my lying down,
and are acquainted with all my ways.

Even before a word is on my tongue,
lo, my Beloved, you know it altogether.
You surround me behind and before,
and lay your hand upon me.
Such knowledge is too wonderful for me;
it is high, I cannot attain it.
Where shall I go from your Spirit?
Where shall I flee from your presence?

If I ascend to heaven you are there!
If I make my bed in Sheol, you are there!
If I take the wings of the morning
and dwell in the uttermost parts of the sea,
even there your hand shall lead me,
and your right hand shall hold me.
If I say, "Let only darkness cover me,
and the light about me be night,"
even the darkness is not dark to you,
the night is bright as the day;
for darkness is as light with you.

For you formed my inward parts,
you knit me together in my mother's womb.
I praise you, for you are fearful and wonderful.

Wonderful are your works!
My soul knows it well;
my body was not hidden from you,
when I was being made in secret,
intricately wrought in the depths of the earth.
Your eyes beheld my unformed substance;
in your book were written, every one of them,
the days that were formed for me,
when as yet there was none of them.

How precious to me are your thoughts, O Beloved!
How vast is the sum of them!
If I would count them, they are more than the sand.
When I awake, I am still with you.
In death I will be with you.

Breathing Light: May all beings feel held in the Light.

Morning Haiku

—*Mary Ann Downey*

morning rituals
oatmeal, milk and tea sprinkled
with a prayer of thanks

called to prayer
singing bowl's voice bids me rest
hear the voice within

lessons in patience
day to day grace sits with me
Calla lily face

recovering walk
each step becomes progress now
snail like adventure

a journey begins
intending to change your life
or maybe one day

—Saint Augustine

Evening Prayer

Watch thou, dear Lord,
with those who wake,
or watch, or weep tonight,
and give thine angels charge
over those who sleep.

Tend thy sick ones, dear Lord.
Rest thy weary ones.
Bless thy dying ones.
Soothe thy suffering ones.
Pity thine afflicted ones.
Shield thy joyous ones.
And all, for thy love's sake.

Bless the Lord
(Benedicite Dominum)

Bless the Lord, all you works of the Lord;
Praise and exalt him above all forever.

Angels of the Lord, bless the Lord;
You heavens, bless the Lord;
All you waters above the heavens, bless the Lord.
All you hosts of the Lord, bless the Lord.

Sun and moon, bless the Lord;
Stars of heaven, bless the Lord.
Every shower and dew, bless the Lord;
All you winds, bless the Lord.

Fire and heat, bless the Lord;
Cold and chill, bless the Lord.

Dew and rain, bless the Lord;
Frost and cold, bless the Lord.

Ice and snow, bless the Lord;
Nights and days, bless the Lord.
Light and darkness, bless the Lord;
Lightning and clouds, bless the Lord.

Let the earth bless the Lord;
Praise and exalt him above all forever.

Mountains and hills, bless the Lord;
Everything growing from the earth, bless the Lord.
You springs, bless the Lord;
Seas and rivers, bless the Lord.

You dolphins and all water creatures, bless the
Lord;
All you birds of the air, bless the Lord.
All you beasts, wild and tame, bless the Lord;
Praise and exalt him above all forever.

You sons of men, bless the Lord;
O Israel, bless the Lord.
Priests of the Lord, bless the Lord;
Servants of the Lord, bless the Lord.

Spirits and souls of the just, bless the Lord;
Holy men of humble heart, bless the Lord.
Ananias, Azarias, Misael, bless the Lord;
Praise and exalt him above all forever.

Let us bless the Father and the Son and the Holy
Ghost;
Let us praise and exalt God above all forever.

Blessed are you in the firmament of heaven;
Praiseworthy and glorious forever.

> **Breathing Light:** Inhale, "I am blessed."
> Exhale, "Forever and ever." Where do you
> recognize the Lord's blessings?

Light of Allah

—*The Qur'an*

llah guides him who will follow His pleasure into the ways of safety and brings them out of utter darkness into light by His will and guides them to the right path.

Allah is the light of the heavens and the earth; a likeness of His light is as a niche in which is a lamp, the lamp is in a glass, and the glass is as it were a brightly shining star, lit from a blessed olive-tree, neither eastern nor western, the oil whereof almost gives light though fire touch it not—light upon light—Allah guides to His light whom He pleases, and Allah sets forth parables for men, and Allah is cognizant of all things.

O you who believe! remember Allah, remembering frequently, and glorify Him morning and evening. He it is who sends His blessings on you, and so do His angels, that He may bring you forth out of utter darkness into the light; and He is merciful to the believers. Their salutation on the day that they meet Him shall be peace, and He has prepared for them an honorable reward. O Prophet! surely we have sent you as a witness, and as a bearer of good news and as a warner, and as one inviting to Allah by His permission, and as a light-giving torch. And give to the believers the good news that they shall have a great grace from Allah.

❖

Breathing Light: Inhale, "Allah guides us to His light." Exhale, "Allah brings us grace and peace." Where do you find Allah's clear light?

The Lord's Prayer

(Aramaic Translation)

Oh Thou, from whom the breath of life comes,
who fills all realms of sound, light and vibration.

May your light be experienced in my utmost holiest.
Your heavenly domain approaches.
Let your will come true—in the universe just as on earth.

Give us wisdom for our daily need,
detach the fetters of faults that bind us,
like we let go the guilt of others.

Let us not be lost in superficial things,
but let us be freed from what keeps us
from our true purpose.

From you comes the all-working will,
the lively strength to act, the song that beautifies all
and renews itself from age to age.

Sealed in trust, faith and truth.
I confirm with my entire being.

Breathing Light: May all beings experience the breath of life.

To Smell the Dhamma

—Ian McCrorie

To smell the Dhamma is to inhale a cloud.
To see the Dhamma is to glimpse night's shadow.
To hear the Dhamma is to listen to the mountain's song.
To touch the Dhamma is to feel the breath of summer rain.
To taste the Dhamma is to sip the dew from a lotus.

Difficult indeed is it to find the proper words to capture the Dhamma.
It cannot be expressed but it can be experienced.

Breathing Light: I am the Dhamma.

Mom's Passing

—Marian Monahan

Her breath bowed low
and with reverence,
recedes into stillness.
She rests at peace,
her fretful heart released,
relaxed, let go.
We witness it,
and hold her in the Mystery
as we say goodbye.
And in a moment,
a life, her life,
which seemed so familiar
and permanent,
is gone.

Death . . .
One of many that day
I'm sure
but ours to behold
and hers to own.
Passing into a place unknown,
that exists in faith
and is spoken of
in the language of hope.

Let Us Not Cling to Mourning

—*Native American Prayer*

Let us not cling to mourning.
Do not stand on my grave and weep.
I am not there, I do not sleep.
I am a thousand winds that blow,
I am the diamond glints on snow,
I am the sunlight opened grain,
I am the gentle autumn rain.

When you awaken in the morning's hush
I am the swift uplifting rush
of quiet birds in a circled flight,
I am the soft stars that shine at night.
Do not stand on my grave and cry.
I am not there, I did not die.

Works of Your Hands

— Traditional Jewish Prayer

How wonderful, O Lord, are the works of
your hands!
The heavens declare your glory,
the arch of the sky displays your handiwork.
In your love you have given us the power
to behold the beauty of your world
robed in all its splendor.

The sun and the stars, the valleys and the hills,
the rivers and the lakes all disclose your presence.
The roaring breakers of the sea tell of your
awesome might,

the beasts of the field and the birds of the air
bespeak your wondrous will.

In your goodness you have made us able to hear
the music of the world.
The voices of the loved ones
reveal to us that you are in our midst.
A Divine voice sings through all creation.

❖

Breathing Light: May all beings hear a
Divine voice.

Bardo Poem

—Roshi Joan Halifax

Beloved Friend
You have now passed through
this breath, this body

Know this: The world through which I speak is a
mirage
All that appears to you now
of and from this realm is insubstantial
Fine and loose as smoke, all that seems solid is
dissolving

Beloved Friend
One hundred thousand fireflies disappear into a
candle's flame

Beloved Friend
This light pervades the infinite expanse with a cool
dark luminosity
Vastness rises into brilliance, recedes into darkness
then encompasses space with the great and clear
light of predawn

Beloved Friend
Only observe the gates of the dissolving elements
You are nothing now but pure compassion and
love

This is the Truth
You Mother Body of vibrant transparent emptiness
You Father body of brilliant ecstatic awareness
press against each other, dissolve into each other
in the orgasmic bliss of ultimate goodness

Beloved Friend
You are now undivided
Your awareness and this infinite joyful vastness
can now be recognized as one
You are free from death and birth
changelessness is present in this purity
that is inherently you

Beloved Friend
Recognize your innate freedom
You are already and have forever been this great
light

Beloved Friend
Recognize your body as the whole body
of unconditioned compassion and love

❖

Breathing Light: May all beings be
liberated.

Prayer for Protection

—*James Dillet Freeman*

The light of God surrounds us;
The love of God enfolds us;
The power of God protects us;
The presence of God watches over us.
Wherever we are, God is.
And all is well.

You Are My Shepherd
(Psalm 23)

My Beloved, you are my shepherd, I shall not want;
you lay me down in lush meadows.
You lead me alongside tranquil waters;
and you restore my soul.
You lead me on the path of blamelessness
in your image.

Even though I walk through the valley
of the shadow of death,
I fear not, for you are with me;
your protection comforts me.
You prepare a table before me
in the presence of my suffering;
you anoint my head and heart with your love,
my cup overflows.

Surely goodness and mercy shall follow me
now and forever;
and I shall dwell with you eternally.

Breathing Light: May all beings sense protection and comfort.

Giver
of Life

—The Bhagavad Gita

O God! You are the giver of life,
the healer of pains and sorrows,
the giver of happiness.
O creator of the universe
send us your purifying light
and lead our thoughts in your ways.

You are the primal God,
the ancient being,
you are the supreme refuge
of the universe,
you are the knower and
the one to be known,
you are the supreme goal,
the universe is pervaded by you.

These bodies of the embodied one,
who is eternal, indestructible, and boundless,
are known as finite.

The embodied one is not born,
nor does he die, nor having been,
ceases he any more to be;
unborn, perpetual, eternal, and ancient,
he is not slain when the body is slaughtered.

As a man, casting worn-out garments,
takes new ones, so the dweller in the body,
casting off worn-out bodies,
enters into others that are new.

For certain is death for the born,
and certain is birth for the dead;
therefore over the inevitable
thou should not grieve.

Journey

—Kendall Dana Lockerman

In the cold, dark rain
Of winter's morning
Slogging in the mud
Scuffing along the road
Scratching against
The rough edges of
This tiresome journey
Of body and soul
A light shines faintly
In a doorway
A warm room with smiles
Voices implore
This is home, for now
Stay as long as you like
There is no destination
Only the journey
Welcome

Spirit of God

—Saint Augustine

Breathe in me, Spirit of God,
that I may think what is holy;

drive me, Spirit of God,
that I may do what is holy;

draw me, Spirit of God,
that I may love what is holy;

strengthen me, Spirit of God,
that I may preserve what is holy;

guard me, Spirit of God,
that I may never lose what is holy.

Karaniya Metta Sutta

—The Buddha's Words on Loving-Kindness

This is what should be done
By one who is skilled in goodness,
And who knows the path of peace:

Let them be able and upright,
Straightforward and gentle in speech,
Humble and not conceited,
Contented and easily satisfied,
Unburdened with duties and frugal in their ways.

Peaceful and calm and wise and skillful,
Not proud or demanding in nature.

Let them not do the slightest thing
That the wise would later reprove.
Wishing: In gladness and in safety,
May all beings be at ease.

Whatever living beings there may be;
Whether they are weak or strong, omitting none,
The great or the mighty, medium, short or small,
The seen and the unseen,
Those living near and far away,
Those born and to-be-born—
May all beings be at ease!

Let none deceive another,
Or despise any being in any state.
Let none through anger or ill-will
Wish harm upon another.

Even as a mother protects with her life
Her child, her only child,
So with a boundless heart
Should one cherish all living beings;
Radiating kindness over the entire world,
Spreading upwards to the skies,
And downwards to the depths;
Outwards and unbounded,
Freed from hatred and ill-will.

Whether standing or walking, seated or lying down
Free from drowsiness,
One should sustain this recollection.
This is said to be the sublime abiding.

By not holding to fixed views,
The pure-hearted one, having clarity of vision,
Being freed from all sense desires,
Is not born again into this world.

Prayer for the Dead

—Hazrat Inayat Kahn

O Thou, the cause and effect of
the whole universe, the source
from whence we have come and
the goal toward which all are
bound: receive this soul who
is coming to Thee into Thy
parental arms.

May Thy forgiving glance heal
our heart. Lift us from the
denseness of the earth, surround
us with the light of Thine own
spirit. Raise us to heaven, which
is our true dwelling place.

We pray Thee grant the blessing
of Thy most exalted presence.
May life upon earth become
as a dream to the waking soul,
and let thirsting eyes behold the
glorious vision of Thy sunshine.

Amen

Blessed Are
(Sermon on the Mount)

Blessed are the poor in spirit:
for theirs is the kingdom of
heaven.
Blessed are they that suffer:
for they shall be comforted.

Blessed are the meek:
for they shall inherit the earth.
Blessed are they who hunger
and thirst for the Beloved:
for they shall be filled.
Blessed are the merciful:
for they shall obtain mercy.
Blessed are the pure in heart:
for they shall see God.
Blessed are the peacemakers:
for they shall be called the
children of God.
Blessed are they who are
steadfast in the Beloved:
for theirs is the kingdom of
heaven.

❖

Breathing Light: May
all beings feel blessed.

Holy Acceptance

—Mary Ann Downey

Thoughts scatter like clouds
blown by the wind, wandering,
wondering where to
rest or fly or dance with this
fresh sparkling morning sunlight.

How can we know what
each day may bring? We wake with
hopeful expectation,
then ask for the grace to hold
and accept whatever comes.

Opening slowly
a white amaryllis greets me.
One called by the light
to stand in praise of this
holy, green golden morning.

❖

Thou Dost Not Fall

—Scottish Gaelic Prayer

As the rain hides the stars,
as the autumn mist
hides the hills,
as the clouds veil
the blue of the sky, so
the dark happenings of my lot
hide the shining of thy face from me.

Yet, if I may hold thy hand in the
darkness,
it is enough, since I know,
that though I may stumble in my going,
thou dost not fall.

Canticle of Brother Sun and Sister Moon

—St. Francis of Assisi

Most high, all-powerful, all-good Lord,
All praise is yours, all glory,
all honor and all blessings.
To you alone, most high, do they belong,
and no mortal lips are worthy to pronounce your
name.

Praised be you, my Lord, with all your creatures,
especially brother sun, who is the day
through whom you give us light.
And he is beautiful and radiant with great
splendor, of you most high, he bears the likeness.

Praised be you, my Lord, through sister moon
and the stars, in the heavens you have made them
bright, precious and fair.

Praised be you, my Lord, through brothers wind
and air, and fair and stormy, all weather's moods,
by which you cherish all that you have made.

Praised be you, my Lord, through sister water,
so useful, humble, precious and pure.

Praised be you, my Lord, through brother fire,
through whom you light the night
and he is beautiful and playful and robust and
strong.

Praised be you, my Lord, through mother earth
who sustains and governs us,
producing varied fruits with colored flowers and
herbs.

Praised be you, my Lord, through those
who grant pardon for love of you and bear sickness
and trial. Blessed are those who endure in peace,
by you most high.

Praised be you, my Lord, through sister death,
from whom no-one living can escape.
Woe to those who die in mortal sin!
Blessed are they she finds doing your will.
No second death can do them harm.

Praise and bless, my Lord, and give him thanks,
and serve him with great humility.

Breathing Light: May all beings benefit
from praise.

Peace Prayer

—Saint Francis of Assisi

Lord, make me an instrument of thy peace;
where there is hatred, let me sow love;
where there is injury, pardon;
where there is doubt, faith;
where there is despair, hope;
where there is darkness, light;
and where there is sadness, joy.

O Divine Master,
grant that I may not so much seek
to be consoled as to console;
to be understood, as to understand;
to be loved, as to love;
for it is in giving that we receive,
it is in pardoning that we are pardoned,
and it is in dying that
we are born to eternal life.

For My Epitaph

—*Steven J. Gold*

On to the full realization of all Paradox:

The simultaneous existence
Of Silence and Sound
Of Darkness and Light
Of Stillness and Perpetual Motion
Of Birth, Life, and Death
Where have I gone?
There is nowhere to go.

There is only
The circle, the spiral
Of energy
Rising,
Transforming,
Dissolving.

There is only Love.

❖

Breathing Light:
May all beings
experience love.

End Notes

Loving-kindness Practice

Loving-kindness, or Metta, meditation helps clarify that there is no separation between you and your loved one. We are all connected and belong to a grand oneness. Comprehending this is particularly important at the end of life. When a loved one dies, the connection between you and your loved one persists.

By practicing loving-kindness, we learn to expand the capacity of our hearts to open toward greater self-awareness and to nurture this oneness. We become better able to acknowledge who we are and learn to fully accept ourselves, integrating all aspects of our experiences—those we consider both positive and negative—into our whole being. Appreciating ourselves allows us to embrace others and to recognize all goodness and difficulties as part of the richness of life. Acceptance fosters our sense of connection.

Through loving-kindness we become increasingly forgiving, forging our capacity to bestow compassion. Forgiveness encourages us to shift our focus from ourselves back to a state of mind that supports the oneness of all. Compassion enables us to bear witness to suffering and have empathy for all beings. Compassionate acts begin by sensing from within what it must be like to undergo someone else's experience.

Metta practice begins with cultivating loving-kindness for oneself, then loving-kindness toward loved ones, friends, community, strangers, those we struggle with, and, finally, all sentient beings. The Metta practice can be profoundly moving as a method to cultivate forgiveness, compassion, and love, and to sense connection. I have found this meditation to align my heart, mind, and soul into a unified, beneficent force. I am able to cultivate the resources required to energetically hold others and me in a state of wellbeing. This leads me to an actively engaged connection with the Beloved in all. It encourages a dynamic commitment both to those I am with and to the greater world.

Reciting the Metta Prayers

Begin by sitting and making any slight adjustments to your posture so that you are comfortable. Start with the first prayer, which offers loving-kindness to yourself. (If you find that it is too difficult to begin with yourself, start with the second prayer, which offers loving-kindness to a loved one.) After each offered prayer, have a moment of silence.

May I be happy.
May I be well.
May I be safe.
May I be peaceful and at ease.

May you be happy.
May you be well.
May you be safe.
May you be peaceful and at ease.

As you continue the meditation, you can bring to mind other loved ones, friends, neighbors, people with whom you struggle, and finally all beings.

The Tonglen meditation teaches us to have compassion for ourselves and for others. It is often easy to feel kindness towards those we love and cherish, especially if we are feeling happy and content ourselves. However, it can be very difficult to feel open and loving towards those we struggle with, fear, or experience as painful. To care about all people who are suffering, we need to embrace our discomfort rather than run from it. By opening our heart, releasing our own tensions, and feeling the discomfort, we can connect with the suffering of that person and within ourselves and awaken compassion for all.

The Tonglen practice teaches us to breath in another's pain to create spaciousness for them, and to breath out whatever would bring them relief and happiness. For example, if a loved one is dying, you, your family, your friends, and the dying person may all be suffering. As you inhale, imagine embracing all of that suffering, trusting your body will transform the pain into love. As you exhale, visualize sending healing, relaxing light and happiness to those in need. Tonglen can be done for those who are ill, those who are dying or have just died, or for those that are in pain of any kind. You may wish to include it in a formal meditation or practice Tonglen in the moment whenever you encounter suffering. The meditation can be envisioned for any number of beneficiaries, even the entire world.

Instructions:

Tonglen in the moment—inhale pain, exhale relief and happiness.

Tonglen as meditation:
- » First, rest your mind in stillness, and open yourself to receive spaciousness and clarity.
- » Second, tune into physical sensations. Breathe in a feeling of hot, dark, and heavy and breathe out a feeling of cool, bright, and light using all the pores of your body.
- » Third, work with any painful situation that is real to you and may be creating an obstacle. Inhale the pain and exhale liberation.
- » Finally, enlarge the "taking in of suffering and sending out of relief and happiness" beyond yourself—to include your loved ones, friends, difficult people, and all beings.

Over time, your ability to be compassionate and your resiliency for holding suffering will expand and strengthen.

❖

Index of Images

David Foster's images can be viewed and pur-chased at *www.davidfosterimages.net*.

Permissions

"Journey" by Kendall Dana Lockerman, from *Rain*, ©2013. Reprinted with permission.

"For My Epitaph" by Steven J. Gold, from *IVRI: The Essence of Hebrew Spirituality, 21st Century Perspectives on an Ancient Tradition*, ©2010. Reprinted with permission.

"Karaniya Metta Sutta: The Buddha's Words on Loving-Kindness" (Sn 1.8), translated from the Pali by The Amaravati Sangha. Amaravati Publications ©2014, *www.amaravati.org*. Reprinted with permission.

"To Smell the Dhamma" by Ian McCrorie, from *The Moon Appears When the Water is Still: Reflections of the Dhamma*, ©2003. Reprinted with permission.

❖

About the Author

Julie Hliboki is the author of *Replenish: Thirty-Three Openings to the Sacred, Cultivating Compassion in an Interfaith World: 99 Meditations to Embrace the Beloved*, and *The Breath of God: Thirty-Three Invitations to Embody Holy Wisdom*. She also has designed and produced a deck of *Compassion Meditation Cards* for inspiration and prayer.

Julie's ministry as a Quaker interfaith chaplain is recorded by the Atlanta Friends Meeting. In addition to hospice and hospital chaplaincy, she works with individuals and groups to deepen their experience of the Light.

Julie holds a Doctor of Ministry, a Master's degree in Transformation Studies, a graduate certificate in Holistic Healthcare, and certifications in professional coaching and expressive arts education. She lives with her beloved, David Addiss, in Atlanta.

For more information, please visit: *www.JulieHliboki.com*.

About the Photographer

David Foster is an award-winning nature photographer whose images have been viewed in more than 50 regional, national, and international exhibitions. Most recently, David won the 2014 P.C. Turczyn Award. In announcing the award, Turczyn wrote: "In selecting a winner, I was looking for beauty, communication, presence, skill, originality, and a full body experience of healing . . . Award winner David Foster's work excels in each of these areas."

The Atlanta Friends Meeting affirms David's work as a recorded ministry. The Meeting wrote: "In sharing his gifts, David invites and inspires viewers to be aware of and engage with the natural beauty they encounter along their existing paths so as to experience it more fully and deeply. Through his exhibitions, David's ministry offers a point of access to nature that opens up for viewers a momentary connection to their soul space."

David's photographs are held in private and public collections globally. For more information, please visit: *www.davidfosterimages.net*.

CPSIA information can be obtained at www.ICGtesting.com
Printed in the USA
BVIW12n0457050215
385939BV00001B/2